FOREX DAY TRADING

s

A Practical Guide to Day Trading Technique for Consistent Profit

Abraham Robert. C

In order to say thank you for purchasing this book, I offer the below video course and more to you as a token of appreciation

Find the Link to the bonus video courses at the end of the book

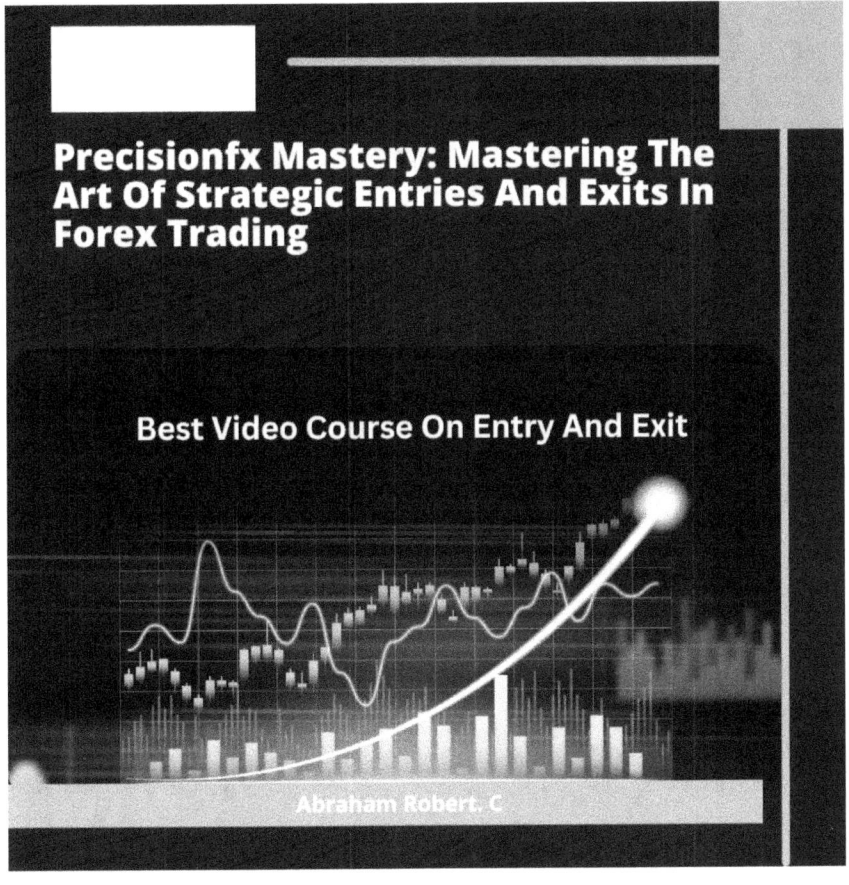

TABLE OF CONTENT

CHAPTER ONE

Overview of Forex Day Trading

Buying and selling assets over a brief time period is known as day trading. Any money, commodity, or financial security that an economic actor bought is referred to as an asset in this context. Traders are market players who engage in trading activities.

It is possible to distinguish between institutional and retail traders. A trader that works independently for oneself is referred to as a retail trader.

A trader who works for a financial institution (such as a commercial bank, investment bank, or hedge fund) and whose duties include trading is known as an institutional trader.

Investing is not the same as trading. Investing is the process of buying assets with the intention of progressively increasing the asset's value over time. A variety of assets may be bought by the market participant, who may then hold the portfolio of assets for a while. The economic agent's objective is to weather short-term price swings and gradually generate a positive return3 over time, even if the portfolio's asset prices may change over time.

Those who participate in the market and practice investing are commonly referred to as investors.

Traders aim to generate profits over a shorter timeframe, typically within a few weeks or days, whereas investors aim for a return within a range of 5% to 15% over a year. Traders attempt to profit on assets' transient price changes.

They aim to purchase assets and sell them for a few dollars or cents more when they execute deals. On the other hand, they trade a lot of assets in each deal, which allows them to earn handsomely.

Traders can be divided into groups according on how they trade. Different trading styles will be discussed in the following section.

Day trading is a type of speculative trading in which a position is opened and closed in the same day.

Suppose you initiate a fresh position at 10 AM and close it by 2 PM on the same day. In such case, you have executed a day trade. That identical position would no longer qualify as a day trade if you closed it the next morning.

In order to attempt to earn money quickly, day traders, also known as active traders, usually employ technical analysis along with a trading plan. They also frequently utilize margin to boost their purchasing power.

Taking advantage of minor price changes during the day in order to cancel all open positions before the market closes is the main objective of day trading.

During a single trading day, it entails purchasing and selling financial products like forex, stocks, options, or crypto currency.

I will give a thorough explanation of many day trading tactics, the dangers involved in day trading, and the possible rewards that successful day traders may experience in this book.

You can decide if day trading is the right trading style for you and how to approach it responsibly and profitably by being aware of the ups and down in day trading method of trading.

In order to succeed in day trading, you need constantly have a trade strategy. The approach must to be an objective one that has been demonstrated to regularly result in greater financial gains than losses. One of two things might be the cause of a retail trader's poor trading performance, even after learning the basics of the financial markets: either the trading strategy is flawed, or the trader is not following the plan. Retail traders who trade without a strategy may find it difficult to distinguish between what is right and incorrect on a systematic basis. As a result, the trader might not be able to systemically fix their prior trading mistakes.

A strategy does not ensure success. Its performance, nevertheless, can be assessed, and adjusted in the end to assist the retail dealer in being successful the marketplace.

A trader may occasionally execute a profitable transaction despite ignoring their trade strategy. While this may provide temporary gratification, over time making random transactions might have a negative impact on a trader's capacity to keep your discipline throughout time.

One way to think about trading as being similar to completing a marathon in that it calls for consistent long-term discipline trading strategy to continuously provide a long-term positive return prosperous entrepreneurs get great prosperity by only grasping the law of averages to ultimately be advantageous to them.

The retail trade should create a trading plan by developing a plan that works for them, their inclination for different technological instruments and level of risk tolerance. The application of trading tactics that are incompatible with the character and profile of the market participant will significantly reduce their likelihood of success.

How to start day trading

The cost and complexity of day trading have been significantly decreased by commission-free online broker accounts. In the past, you needed to phone a stockbroker to complete a deal. This greatly raised the cost of each contract in addition to being very time-consuming. Moreover, inexperienced investors have difficulty accessing market data.

These days, the best online brokerages, like Interactive Brokers or Trade Station, allow you to trade quickly and cheaply from the comfort of your home. Most do not impose fees on trading stocks, ETFs, or a variety of other assets. They also provide a ton of thorough market data for free.

As soon as your brokerage account is established, you will be able to buy and sell assets. Numerous research tools, such as stock screeners, scanners, market news, and charts, would also be available to you.

As a day trader, you choose the markets and assets you want to focus on. In order to benefit from positions that you time, you then try to buy and sell at the appropriate times of day. For example, you may buy a stock just before an announcement pushes up the price, and then sell when you think the price has peaked.

CHAPTER TWO

Trading Methods

In summary, trading approaches may be divided into four groups:

1. Position
2. Swing
3. Scalping
4. Day trading.

Position trading is the practice of an economic actor holding a position for a few weeks to many months. Initially, position traders look for patterns in asset prices. Should they anticipate a positive trend, they would invest in the asset long. They could short sell the asset if they notice a negative trend.

Position traders attempt to ride the "wave" of a well-established trend and profit from the general movement of a commodity in a market, rather than necessarily attempting to foresee the future pricing of the asset. When the trend breaks, position traders usually exit their position.

Typically, positional traders aim to profit from the most favorable portion of an asset's movement when it follows a long-term trend. The majority of assets, including stocks, exhibit a price movement pattern driven by a notable shift in the underlying fundamentals. Nonetheless, certain assets take a long time to move due to significant shifts in the industry or the asset's inherent fundamentals. The asset price will move at an increased rate for several weeks or months before stopping if these changes have an impact on the industry's long-term prospects. Typically, positional traders aim to profit from the most favorable portion of an asset's movement when it follows a long-term trend.

The majority of assets, including stocks, exhibit a price movement pattern driven by a notable shift in the underlying fundamentals. Nonetheless, certain assets take a long time to move due to significant shifts in the industry or the asset's inherent fundamentals.

The asset price will move at an increased rate for several weeks or months before stopping if these changes have an impact on the industry's long-term prospects.

A trader can select his deals according to his skill set even if positional trading does not have any established tactics. In general, traders are naturally skilled in technical analysis. Nonetheless, some traders go above and beyond to master fundamental research, utilizing both technical and fundamental analysis to generate profits from trading.

Position trading strategies

Technical Strategy

A technical technique looks exclusively at charts to identify the asset price's long-term trend. Trades begin when the asset price exhibits long-term trend behavior. Generally, it evaluates the asset's price, volume, and relative strength. This trading is entirely based on price movements; no fundamental reasons are taken into account.

Fundamental Strategy

A fundamental approach places greater focus on the underlying elements influencing an asset's price.

The strategy searches for a structural change in the underlying business environment and solely takes into account qualitative factors.

The trader may operate with far more confidence when using the basic approach as opposed to trading only on technicalities, which is one of its main advantages.

Techno-Fundamental Strategy

Technical and fundamental analysis are used by a trader to make inform trading choices. Charts are used to examine price behavior and confirm fundamentals in order to assess long-term qualitative changes. The trade executes if the price changes in line with the shift in the fundamentals.

Swing trading

Those who have full-time employment or are enrolled in school and have enough spare time to keep up with global economic developments are the ideal candidates for swing trading.

Swing traders also use technical or fundamental research to predict if the price of a certain currency pair will rise or fall in the near future.

Scalping

Scalping is sometimes defined as a kind of day trading strategy that involves several trades with extremely brief holding times, perhaps as little as a few seconds or minutes. Because positions are held for such short times, there is little benefit from any one transaction (or profit per trade). In order to make money, scalpers execute a large number of deals, perhaps as many as hundreds, in a typical trading day.

In order to match the frequency of trading, scalpers search for sufficient liquidity. These traders need to be able to execute deals fast and have access to correct data (such as a quotation system). Direct brokerage access is often favored since high fees raise the cost of completing transactions, which reduces earnings on frequent buys and sells.

It's important to remember that scalping works best for people that have the patience, attention, and fast thinking. It's a prevalent belief that those who lack patience are effective scalpers since they prefer to get out of a deal as soon as it starts to earn money. Scalping is best suited for people who can manage tension, respond promptly, and make judgment calls.

Scalping is a faster kind of range trading where the goal is to buy and sell an investment at small price changes. To try to earn a little profit on every tiny movement, a scalping day trader may buy and sell hundreds of times a day for a single investment. Scalpers keep an eye on short-term price charts to try to spot these patterns.

Day trading strategy

When you day trade, you use a method to identify profitable assets. A number of frequently used strategies include the following.

Trading the News

Day traders actively watch the news in order to benefit from market volatility before to significant events, such as the publication of the most recent jobs report or a Federal Reserve interest rate increase.

They search for assets that, in the wake of a major news event, have not yet completely reprised or attempt to predict the direction in which asset prices will move.

This approach also works well when traders follow the news flow for certain asset classes or individual stocks. Trading a publicly listed company is usual both before and after the company's quarterly earnings report is released.

Trading Range market

Finding assets that regularly move within a certain price range is the aim of range trading. The trader wants to buy an investment when the market price is getting close to the low end of the range, and he wants to sell it when it is close to the high end.

When range trading, timing is crucial, and poor order execution may result in significant losses. Unexpected news or market events might break the price ranges, which could lead to quick or unfavorable price swings.

Momentum Trading

For stocks and other assets, there are often general price trends. A stock may keep losing money if more investors sell their shares if it begins to lose money one day. On the other hand, if additional investors follow the pattern, a firm that has been increasing in value may continue to do so.

Momentum investors try to take advantage of these price patterns by basing their strategy on the notion that past price fluctuations may be a reliable indicator of future developments. Momentum traders often utilise technical indicators and chart patterns to help them decide when to join and exit a trade.

Fading

When fading, a day trader takes a contrarian stance. The trader makes investments in assets that have undergone significant liquidation or sells assets that have increased in value. A trader using a fading approach expects the herd mentality to cause prices to go too far in either direction.

The goal is to profit from market overreactions to news or occurrences. Traders think pricing will eventually bring us to the mean. However, since it veers from the dominant trend, fading might be a dangerous strategy that can result in losses if it takes the market some time to achieve equilibrium levels.

Leverage

For day traders, leverage is a frequent investment approach. Trading with borrowed money and using margin are required for this. Margin trading provides a considerably higher potential rewards if your trades are successful, but it also has a much higher loss rate. Your broker may also charge interest on margin loans.

CHAPTER THREE

Advantages and Disadvantages of Day trading

Buying and selling assets on the same day is known as day trading. Positions are not retained for a long time. The same day, every position is closed. By taking advantage of an asset's price volatility within a single day, day traders aim to benefit.

Day traders make money by trading a lot of securities, just like scalpers do. The trading window for day traders is throughout the trading day's busy hours, whereas the trading window for scalpers is between a few seconds and a few minutes.

The size of their trading account, their degree of expertise, the amount of time they are willing to spend to trading, and their risk tolerance are the factors that traders consider when choosing their trading strategy.

All open positions are typically closed before the end of a trading session, and these positions are never left open for more than a day. Proficient day traders won't just select a stock or currency pair at random and try to trade it on a given day. They will identify opportunities to benefit from the financial markets quickly and frequently by using day trading tactics and research.

It's possible that day traders might try to make several deals on the same asset in one day. Finding advantageous entry and exit opportunities in the markets that allow day traders to take little, consistent returns from frequently minute market moves is crucial. It takes a lot of discipline and effort to day trade.

Making tiny but many returns on moderate price movements over the course of a day is the idea behind day trading.

Leverage provided by brokers is another tool that day traders will employ. With the use of leverage, traders may expand their total market exposure to two, even four times, the amount of their original investment.

It increases losses when open positions don't perform as expected by traders, but it also helps to maximize lucrative day trading positions.

Advantages of day trading

If one is successful in day trading, the advantages may well exceed the risks. Day trading requires focus and time management, but it also allows someone to choose their own hours without having a boss or company monitor them. In addition to offering the opportunity to make a sizable income from the comforts of one's home, day trading has further advantages over more traditional approaches to stock and financial instrument trading.

Potential for quick financial gain

Every decision you make as a day trader might result in profit. If every deal you make becomes a profit—and that's a big if—you may accumulate riches far more quickly than the typical investor. The lucrative potential of day trading is often emphasized in online courses that support it.

Easy to get to

With today's sophisticated brokerage platforms, day trading is much simpler than it was in the past. You may set things up using your home computer and smartphone.

It's not boring

Investing in buy-and-hold securities lacks the exhilaration that comes with day trading. When you put in the work, spot an opportunity, and close a deal successfully, you get a thrill. It's not as amazing to tell your dinner party guests that your investment has doubled in size over the last seven years as it is to tell them that you doubled your investment in a day.

Achievement in Unfavorable Market Conditions

Using short-selling trading techniques to profit from declining market prices, day traders may frequently exploit a faltering market. For an experienced day trader, being able to profit from the stock market during a bear market is a huge benefit.

No risk overnight

Typically, day traders exit all of their positions in investments before the market closes for the day. They are so shielded from additional losses at night. Ordinary investors are still holding positions and risk losing money if anything unexpected occurs overnight that prevents them from trading, such as a breaking news story that negatively impacts their portfolio.

The flexibility to terminate your position at the conclusion of the trading day, or earlier, is one of the biggest benefits of day trading. The dangers associated with holding a deal overnight are eliminated for a day trader who opens and closes his position before the trading day finishes. While trading long-term, conventionally, a trader's winnings might vanish overnight. However, while trading day trading, your profits are safe as long as you close your positions before the conclusion of the trading day. If it was a pleasant day, this enables you to get a decent night's sleep.

You are your own boss

Day trading is a source of income for certain professional traders. Should you find this approach enjoyable and effective, it may eventually replace your current career.

Imagine yourself working calmly from home on your computer, making trades, and enjoying a cup of coffee. However, there is one thing missing: the manager or boss who is always hovering over you. You are in the game for yourself; you don't need to ask for permission to trade or comply with demands from other people. In the end, your performance is your own responsibility and accountability. You lose money if you don't succeed; maybe a lot of money. Even while we would all like to have this independence, it does serve as a reminder that you must possess the discipline and work ethic necessary to be well-versed in the industry.

- ✓ It's difficult for individuals who are successful to envision generating more money at practically anything else.
- ✓ Ideal for mobile lives as it can be done from any location with internet access.
- ✓ Employ yourself. Savor your freedom.
- ✓ A successful trader usually works two to three hours a day.
- ✓ Entertaining and mentally stimulating.
- ✓ Quite low overhead
- ✓ Compared to beginning a business or investing in real estate, there is a far lower barrier to entry.

The disadvantages of day trading

High likelihood of losses

A high-risk, high-reward method is day trading. You can lose money far faster than a typical investor if your selections don't pan out, particularly if you employ leverage. 97% of those who day traded for more than 300 days lost money, according to a two-year research involving 1,600 traders. In addition to hard work and knowledge, day trading success also requires a great deal of luck.

Taxes and fees

Even while trading expenses have decreased, there may still be fees associated with some kinds of transactions, particularly when volume is high.

You owe more in taxes than the average investor as well. In contrast to the long-term capital gains rate, you pay a greater tax on short-term capital gains when you sell an investment for a gain after less than a year of ownership.

High-Risk High-Reward

Although most traders acknowledge that intraday trading is among the most lucrative trading strategies, they also acknowledge that it carries the highest level of risk. An intraday trader must have observing abilities and a thorough understanding of the market. Establishing yourself as an intraday trader is difficult, but it gets easier if you know the regulations.

Time-consuming

The art of intraday trading is intricate. Furthermore, you are unable to exit your computer or mobile app before finishing a deal, in contrast to positional or long-term trading. Despite the fact that you can set goals, halt losses, and return to your full-time job, this strategy is not sustainable over the long term. A trade may occasionally hit the stop loss before reaching the aim. Alternately, it can come back and strike the stop loss just a little distance from the target price. By being engrossed in the price movement, you may steer clear of these issues and trade like an expert.

Excessive Volatility Could Unnerve You

A stock may be moving erratically on the 1-, 3-, or 5-minute charts. On the other hand, the motions will appear more streamlined and predictable when you view a daily or 30-minute chart. Therefore, if you dislike volatility, it could be wise to avoid intraday trading.

High stress

The markets change swiftly, and it may be rather frustrating to see your balance fluctuate, particularly if your transactions aren't profitable. Day trading is a type of gambling that may get compulsive and negatively impact your relationships and health.

Time-consuming and challenging

Day trading calls for a large time investment. You must invest hours in market research and strategy development in addition to spending hours tracking and placing transactions.

Making money is particularly difficult as you are up against other investors, including experts employed by big financial organizations.

- ✓ Has a lengthy and steep learning curve
- ✓ Needs a risk-taking mindset.
- ✓ Needs to be assertive and competitive.
- ✓ A fluctuating

What does it take to day trade

Here's everything you need to start day trading if you think you would enjoy to:

• A research tool-equipped brokerage platform. It is better to use some trading platforms for day trading than others. Check out the top online brokers for day traders if you'd like a suggestion.

• Information and abilities. You have to know what you're doing when you make transactions. To choose the day trading tactics you want to employ, you might enroll in a day trading course. You may also enroll in a community college course on investment or business in your area.

• Research and news about markets. Think about the way you'll investigate your deals. Certain systems offer continuous market research. To exchange advice, you might also wish to join online day trading communities or subscribe to newsletters.

• An abundance of time. Choose the time when you can start day trading. You should give it your full attention while markets are open, which is during typical business hours and may interfere with your regular employment.

• The appropriate frame of mind. Think about if you can tolerate temporary losses in exchange for day trading profits. And if you're prepared to work hard for this risky tactic.

Essential Tools for Forex Day Trading

In the currency market alone, traders exchange trillions of dollars every day, and they employ day trading instruments. Every day, hundreds of billions of dollars' worth of trades are made in commodities and stocks.

A large number of new companies have been able to join marketplaces because to technological advancements, in part because of the growth of more widely available technology.

You need a variety of day trading tools to assist you in making wise selections if you want to succeed in any field:

You may improve as a trader and make wiser financial decisions by using the following free day trading tools.

Tools for Charting

Traders want superior charting tools in order to make more informed trading decisions. They can choose when to enter and leave a transaction with the use of these charts.

Some traders find it challenging to use popular trading platforms and tools like Meta trader. They may make more accurate and predictable charts with the aid of additional free tools.

A platform for applying technical indicators and comparing various securities is provided by Yahoo Finance. An competitor to Bloomberg that costs some few amount per month is called Money.net. With a free account, one may use the day trading tool to generate charts and view investor feedback.

You may also utilize Stock Charts, Trading view, and Net Dania as charting tools. We recommend the latter to get things started.

Websites for Financial News

Websites covering financial news are crucial for breaking news and commentary on a range of instruments.

Opinions from individual investors and other opinion makers can be shared on websites like investing.com. Furthermore, the website offers a platform that allows traders to create charts and simultaneously compare prices for many goods. Additionally, the software does real-time technical analysis to assist traders in making wise trading selections.

The Pip Value Estimator

The lowest value a currency may fluctuate is called a pip. It's really difficult to figure out how much a pip is worth. Furthermore, you may download a calculator from the Android or iPhone store to assist you in doing this, so you won't need to perform the computation.

To compute a pip value, simply input the desired currency pair, position size, ask price, and value expressed in US dollars into the calculator. The value of the pip will then be generated.

Pivot Point Estimator

The majority of users of this program are technical traders. Being in a strong position to recognize the pivot point is essential for technical traders. You may find the points of support and resistance by using this pivot point.

To begin with, figuring out these turning points might be a pretty challenging task. The pivot point calculator can help with that. All one needs to do to find all the pivot points is enter the high, low, and close prices into this calculator.

MetaTrader

commonly referred to as MT4/MT5, is one of the top trading platforms globally. The majority of internet brokers provide it.

With the free download of the program, traders may practice trading on a practice account. Additionally, it enables traders to trade real money that has been put through the broker on a genuine account.

The Meta trader is a tool that new traders may use to learn how to trade using real-time data. They can also learn how to design their own trading algorithms and utilize expert advisors. Numerous charting tools, a news feed, and hundreds of technical indicators are among the other tools provided by MetaTrader.

CHAPTER FOUR

Developing a Successful day Trading Strategy

These are the general procedures to follow in order to create a profitable Forex strategy that you can maintain.

First step: What type of trader are you?

Knowing which type of trader you are can help you concentrate your time, attention, and resources on creating Forex trading methods that suit your trading preferences.

For certain traders, there are situations where the most profitable approach may not be a good fit or a losing one for another kind of trader.

Second step: What trading style best describes you?

After completing all of these questions, you will begin to see your place on the trading spectrum. There are several kinds and classifications that you can fall into:

• Preference for a trading timeframe: position, swing, day, or scalper trading

• Preference for a certain sort of trading analysis: fundamental or technical

• A predilection for risk tolerance: loving, neutral, or indifferent to risk

One of four trading type's scalper, day, swing, or position will apply to you.

Day trading and scalping

Given that they both require you to start and liquidate all of your trading positions inside the same trading day, these two forms of trading are the most active and aggressive types of currency trading.

You should consider day trading and scalping if you

• Preferred intraday trading over holding holdings overnight.

• Would like to know if, at the end of the trading day, you made or lost money.

• Accept a significant degree of market risk.

• Have the ability to anticipate market trends and respond swiftly to emerging opportunities.

• Able to handle a fair amount of stress.

• Enjoy quick-paced trading.

Swing Trading

This trading strategy is a medium-term one that relies on capitalizing on shifts in a currency pair's momentum inside the main trend. Typically, traders hold their positions for a few days or a few weeks.

Since you'll be holding your trading positions for several days or weeks at a time, usually with a good amount of leverage, swing trading calls for a lot of patience. Because they don't always have the time to examine the market every day, it's perfect for active part-time traders.

Swing trading is for you if;

• You don't have a lot of daily time to spend in front of screens.

• You have days or weeks to hang onto your positions.

You are partial to technical analysis.

Position Trading

This trading strategy is long-term and focused on profiting from shifts in a currency pair's long-term pricing. Traders can maintain a position for several weeks, months, or even years at a time.

Position traders don't care about the short-term price swings; they take a position and keep it.

These trades are usually placed with moderate leverage or in the currency futures market, where funding is factored in. Position traders aim to spot and profit from significant trends, and they may only conduct their research once a month or so.

If any of the following apply to you, position trading may be right for you:

• You prefer fundamental research;

• You can hang onto your positions for months or years;

• You don't want to employ a lot of leverage.

Your present schedule, attention span, and risk aversion are all important factors to consider when determining which trading style best fits your personality.

As a result, you must align your chosen timeline with your personality and way of living.

One trading strategy for position trading is to use a daily period. When swing trading, you can use 4-hour to daily charts and hold your position for a few days or even weeks. Using tick to hourly charts, you will hold a position with scalping and day trading for a few seconds to a day.

Third step: When making trading decisions, what type of analysis technique will you employ?

A couple different analytical philosophies can work well for your personality. Technical and fundamental traders are the most popular types, but you may also be a market timer, noise trader, mood trader, and arbitrage trader.

Technical traders

Technical analysts examine an asset's price fluctuations using historical data to predict future price changes.

To trade, they employ price pattern analysis, market theory, Japanese candlestick analysis, trend analysis, support and resistance analysis, and mathematical and technical indicators.

Fundamental traders

A financial asset's true value can be ascertained by fundamental traders, who also use these criteria to assess whether an asset is overvalued, undervalued, or should be sold.

A basic Forex trader will mostly employ currency carry or news trading methods, primarily based on changes in interest rates that have the biggest influence on the movement of exchange rates.

Fourth step: How are you going to enter/leave the market?

While sound fundamental analysis reveals the "why," competent technical analysis provides the "when."

We believe that both analytic techniques ought to be applied.

When it comes to timing their entries and exits from the Forex markets, traders often depend on technical analysis. However, they also monitor the economic calendar to stay informed about news that may impact market volatility and present trading chances.

Once you've determined the type of market analysis to use to your trading approach, you need to recognize and comprehend the various market stages. Certain market situations are optimal for specific instruments and indicators.

Knowing your preferred trading circumstances (ranging markets, trending markets, volatile/non-volatile markets, pull-back or breakout phases) will allow you to focus on a particular market phase and become proficient with the trading indicators and tools that are used to detect it.

Alternatively, to further tailor your trade to market circumstances, you might create many trading systems for each of the main market phases rather than just one, utilizing tools like candlestick patterns, technical indicators, and drawing tools.

Define your risk while following sound risk and money management rules

Knowing how much money you're willing to lose on each trading position is the first step in assessing your risk. Being a competent trader requires thinking about losing, which is not an easy task.

Each trader's connection to risk and self-awareness play a role in determining the right amount of risk to take.

You can adhere to basic financial and risk management guidelines like these:

• Use only as much cash as you can afford to lose.

• Take your trading style into account while managing risk.

• Take note of the location size.

• Use limit and stop orders at all times.

Establish a minimum risk/reward ratio of 1:2 (or 1:3, if you're a swing or position trader).

• For any position, you may risk no more than 1% of your available trading capital.

• Don't leverage too much.

Use the proper level of leverage for your trading capital and risk tolerance. Leverage is a terrific instrument to raise your potential earnings, but it also increases your possible losses.

Fifth step: Test your system both forward and backward

After identifying your personality type and preferred trading style, you should test your trading strategy using both historical data (back-testing) and real trading data (forward-testing), as well as current market circumstances.

This will show you which market situations are most profitable and give you greater confidence that you are employing a profitable technique.

Before using real money on a live trading account with your trading technique, it is also sensible to unbiasedly assess its dependability and make any required adjustments to increase its effectiveness.

Back-testing in day trading

The process of evaluating your trading strategy on a collection of historical data as if you were trading at that time with the chosen strategy is known as back-testing.

Forward-testing in day trading

Forward-testing expands the data on which you test your approach by utilizing current data (or "out-of-sample" data), whereas back-testing concentrates on a specific set of data with precise conditions in the past (also known as "in-sample" data).

Forward testing, also known as paper trading, allows you to test your trading system in real-world scenarios without risking real money by using a simulated market environment. It operates by keeping track of every trade purchase and sale decision you would make in accordance with your trading strategy and calculating the "paper" earnings you would have made in actual trading.

Opening a "demo" account, which simulates real-time market and trading circumstances using virtual funds, is one approach to paper trade. From there, you may assess if your technique has the potential to be lucrative.

Paper trading is essential to your trading adventure, regardless of your level of experience. Paper trading is an excellent way for a novice trader to learn the markets and the trading process while advancing without having to risk any real money.

If you are more experienced, paper trading might be a helpful way to improve your trading strategy without risking real money.

Your trading technique has a positive expectation and you would have profited from it at that time if the outcomes are lucrative. You can adjust some of your parameters and run another test to achieve the best potential results.

It's crucial to avoid making too many changes to your variables, though, since this would result in a trading strategy that is highly tailored to the unique market circumstances that come with the exact historical data you utilized. Because of this, it is unlikely that your method would be able to adjust to future price changes.

Day Trading Timeframe

The trading term represented by each candlestick or bar on a price chart is indicated by a timeframe. It represents the amount of time that is included in a single data point, such one minute, five minutes, fifteen minutes, and so on. For traders, timeframes are crucial because they offer a variety of perspectives on market movements and enable a detailed examination of price behavior at different granularities.

Timeframes for Day Trading

The following chart periods are ideal for day trading:

• One-minute: The market action is represented by each candlestick or bar.

• 5-Minute: Five minutes of market action are represented by each candlestick or bar.

• 15-Minute: The market action is shown by each candlestick or bar every fifteen minutes.

• Thirty minutes of market action are represented by each candlestick or bar.

• One-Hour: One hour's worth of market action is represented by each candlestick or bar.

These are the typical times that you will encounter, however there could be additional windows, such three and forty-five minutes.

Ideal Timeframe for Day Trading

The best time frame for day trading mostly depends on the strategy, temperament, and personal preferences of the trader. Scalping and quick trades benefit greatly from the complex and quick price movement that is provided by short periods like one minute and five minutes. This type of trading is mainly preferred by skilled and involved market participants and requires quick decision-making.

On the other hand, swing traders may be better suited to longer periods, such as 15- or 30-minute charts, which allow them to take advantage of more extensive price movements across many hours. These periods require less frequent supervision but nevertheless include trading in the comparatively short-term range.

There isn't a one solution that works for everyone, therefore traders frequently try out several time frames to see what suits them the best. The Tick Trader tool allows you to evaluate different financial products over time.

• For one minute. The goal of trading on a 1-minute chart is for traders to capture little profits from extremely brief price changes. This technique has a high trade frequency, which means it requires a great deal of focus, expertise, and discipline.

• Fifteen minutes. The scalpers also utilize the 5-minute chart. Day traders that seek for rapid price fluctuations within a single session tend to favor it. If traders can get the hang of this fast-paced method, they can be rewarded for their attention and rapid decision-making.

• Fifteen minutes. Trading a 15-minute chart allows you to strike a balance between taking advantage of brief price changes and having adequate time for research and deliberation. It can be useful for swing and scalp traders who would rather hold positions for a few hours rather than deal with the noise of shorter periods.

Trading Across Several Timeframes

Many traders observe the market more thoroughly by utilizing multiple times frame at once. This method is sometimes referred to as multiple timeframe analysis (MTFA). Traders often employ three periods. They trade the medium, use the longest to assess an overall trend with strong support and resistance levels, and use the shortest to assess possible risks before entering or exiting a trade.

Trend and counter trading method of trading

Trading involves more than just picking stocks or currencies at random too long or short.

Trading strategies are usually the foundation of successful traders' profits. In actuality, without a methodical methodology, it is challenging for any trader to consistently produce returns over the long term.

 Different kinds of trading methods exist. Certain trading techniques are easy to understand and may be used by any trader. Some tactics are more advanced and dependent on machinery and computer software.

There isn't really a single response that can be given to describe what the finest and most lucrative Forex trading technique is. The most effective forex techniques will depend on the person. This implies that in order to determine the optimal Forex strategy for you, you must take your personality into account. Something that could be ideal for another person could be disastrous for you.

On the other hand, a tactic that has been rejected by others could work well for you. As a result, finding profitable Forex trading methods may need some trial and error. Those that don't work for you might also be eliminated by it. Setting a timeframe for your trading strategy is one of the most important things to do.

Different trading styles exist, ranging from short-term to long-term strategies. These methods have been employed extensively over the years and are still regarded as some of the greatest forex trading techniques.

In their quest to learn how to trade Forex profitably, the most skilled traders are constantly aware of the many approaches and tactics, enabling them to select the appropriate one based on the condition of the market.

Trend Trailing Forex Techniques

Occasionally, a market breaks out of a range and initiates a trend by rising above or below the resistance. How is this possible? Buyers start to hold off when a market hits new lows and support collapses.

This is a result of purchasers' persistent observation of falling prices and their desire to hold out for the lowest price to be obtained. Simultaneously, some traders will be liquidating their holdings out of fear or will be taking on short positions due to their belief that prices may drop.

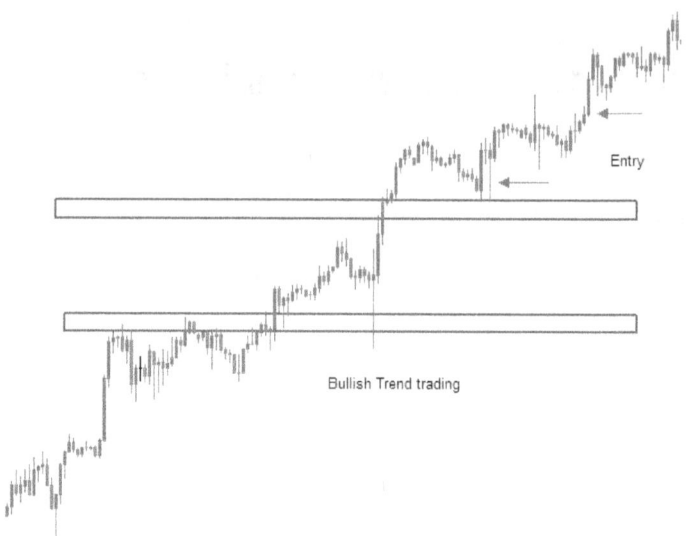

Bullish Trend trading

The pattern keeps on until buyers begin to believe again that the prices won't drop anymore and the selling volume is exhausted. Trend-following methods advise traders to sell a market when it breaks through support and purchase it once it breaks through resistance.

Bearish Trend Trading

Trends may sometimes be both striking and persistent. This kind of methodology might be the most effective Forex trading method due to the size of the changes involved. Although there's no foolproof method to tell, trend-following systems employ indications to alert traders when a new trend could have started.

The good news is that you are increasing your chances of success if the indicator can pinpoint a moment when there is a higher likelihood that a trend has started. A breakout is the sign that a trend may be developing. When the price rises above either the highest high or the lowest low for a predetermined period of days, it is considered a breakout.

Bearish Trend Trading

Entry

Forex Counter-Trend Strategies

Although I don't recommend this trading method, it could be profitable sometimes if you matter how that particular market moves. Counter trend trading is like swimming against the flow of a river, it's much easier to swim in the direction of the flow of a river, so also it's much easier to trend with the trend.

Countertrend tactics are predicated on the observation that the majority of breakouts do not culminate in sustained trends. As a result, a trader employing this technique looks to take advantage of prices' propensity to rebound from past highs and lows. Given their high success rate, counter-trend methods appear to be among the greatest Forex trading tactics for boosting confidence.

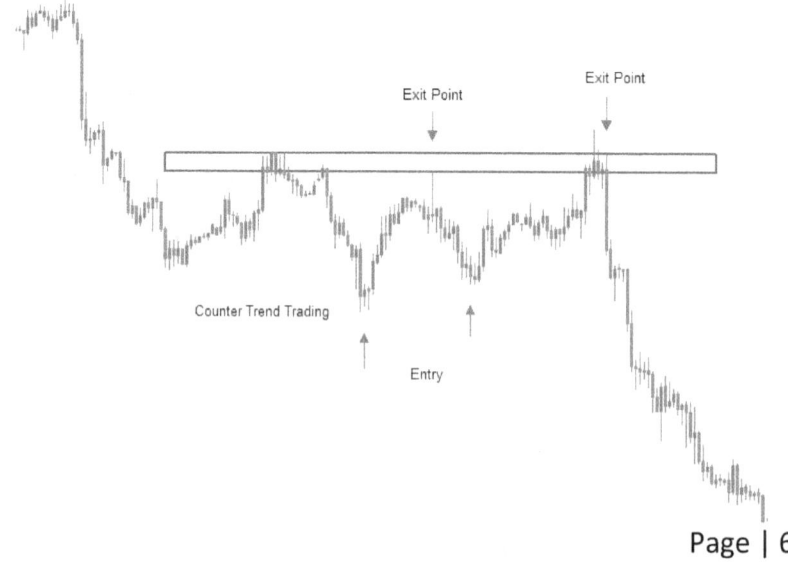

It's crucial to remember that risk management requires strict controls. Support and resistance levels must hold for these Forex trading methods to work. However, if these levels collapse, there's also a chance of significant negative outcomes. It is beneficial to keep an eye on the market regularly.

Stable and tumultuous markets are ideal for this kind of approach. A market setting like this allows for reasonable price movements that stay within a certain range. It's crucial to remember that the market is subject to change.

Risk Assessment

Trading is the art of controlling risk and executing trading strategies. Proficient traders meticulously evaluate and rationalize their risk before committing to a transaction. To put it another way, they must consider the potential loss on each deal they make.

To ensure that their trades are performed at target prices, they could heavily rely on limit orders for opening and closing positions. A trader must be aware of the best times to initiate deals, maintain positions, and leave deals in order to control risk.

A trader would benefit from having this knowledge as it would stop them from selling a successful position too soon, holding a losing position for too long, and jumping into a profitable momentum too late.

Retail traders ought to limit their trading to funds they can afford to lose. It is advised to do this since trading has a risk of financial loss for the trader.

It's not advisable to trade with money that is needed for necessities like food, rent, utilities, medical care, or schooling. In fact, if a retail trader is afraid of losing their money, they can hang onto winning positions for too little time or sell losing positions too soon, which could cause them to realize unwarranted losses.

Naturally, this might lead to a negative profit-to-loss ratio for the individual trader. Therefore, it is advised that until one's financial situation improves, someone who cannot afford to lose the money they risk in trading stick to demo trading.

GET INSTANT ACCESS TO THE FREE VIDEO COURSE BY FOLLOWING THE BELOW LINK

subscribepage.io/freeforexcourse

Click or copy and paste the above link on your browser for instant access to the bonus video.

Happy Trading!